Influencing Virtual Teams

17 Tactics That Get Things Done with Your Remote Employees

By

Hassan Osman

Influencing Virtual Teams: 17 Tactics That Get Things Done With Your Remote Employees
Copyright © 2014 by Hassan Osman.

entirely at your own risk and that you are solely responsible for your use of the contents. The advice of a competent legal counsel (or any other professional) should be sought. The author, company, and publisher do not warrant the performance, effectiveness or applicability of any sites or references listed in this book. Some links are affiliate links. This means that if you decide to make a purchase after clicking on some links, the author will make a commission. All references and links are for information purposes only and are not warranted for content, accuracy or any other implied or explicit purpose.

Table of Contents

Introduction

I intentionally limited the length of this book to less than eighty pages.

Why? Two reasons.

First, I wanted to write a book that *I* wanted to read. No fluff, no filler content, no BS. Just helpful, meaty content that gets you results. You won't find any "definitions" of virtual teams here. Nor will you read about any "statistical trends" on the future of telecommuting.

What you will get is a straightforward list of seventeen tactics that you can immediately use as a guide to influence your virtual team to get things done.

Second, I wanted to focus on the tactics that will give you the maximum return on investment for your time. I could have added fifty more tips to this book, but stuffing more words just to fill up a book with more content would have diluted the potency of the tips presented here.

So don't equate the brevity of this book with a lack of usefulness. On the contrary, you're going to learn some incredibly valuable tactics that will immediately help you manage your remote employees.

Three Reasons Why You Need This Book

If you manage a virtual team, there are three powerful reasons why you need this book.

Reason 1: You'll Get Tactics, Not Just Strategies

Strategies don't mean anything unless they can be immediately applied. You can listen to strategic advice such as "build a culture of trust" or "encourage social interactions among your team" all day long. But if you don't get specific *tactical* steps that you can implement straightaway, those strategies won't be of much help.

This book focuses on actionable tips that show you exactly how to apply these management techniques with your team. You'll also get some great examples that help reinforce those tactics for you.

Reason 2: Science-Backed Research

I'm a strong believer in a science-based approach to management. I'm also a voracious reader of non-fiction books—particularly books about influence, psychology, productivity, and management.

For this book, I've gathered some of the best ideas I've learned from all those sources and included them here for you. So the tactics you'll learn are backed by proven scientific studies that have been published in best-selling books such as *Influence: The Psychology of*

Persuasion and top-notch journals such as the *Harvard Business Review.*

All those sources are included in the footnotes.

Reason 3: Practical Advice From Someone Who Does This for a Living

You may ask, "Who is Hassan Osman and why should I listen to him?"

Good question. For over ten years I've been managing and researching virtual teams. I teach a course about managing virtual teams, I blog about working from home, and I frequently publish articles about remote work. I've done everything from managing small three-member teams as an entrepreneur to leading large-scale implementations with over thirty remote workers as a project manager in a Fortune 100 company.

Currently, I'm a senior program manager at Cisco Systems, where I lead virtual teams all over the world on delivering complex projects. (Important note: the opinions expressed in this book are my own views, and not those of Cisco).

At any given point in time, I could be managing a team of employees in more than eight different countries. I also manage multiple projects with multiple customers in different time zones. I don't say all that to brag, but I do want you to realize that I eat and breathe this topic on a daily basis. My company depends on me to know my business, and if I didn't get results from my teams, I'd be out of a job.

Over the years, I've gained a lot of insights about what

works and what doesn't with virtual teams. Some ideas are based on my own self-experimentation, while others are based on data-driven and scientific studies.

This book contains the best of the best practical advice that I learned which will help you get things done with your virtual team. I guarantee it.

Your Free Bonus

As a thank-you for your purchase, I'm offering a free bonus that is exclusive to my readers.

The bonus includes two templates to help you with your meetings: a **meeting agenda template** and a **meeting minutes template** that you can use for your own team (I'll explain how to use those templates in Tactics 13 and 14 of this book). The templates are in Microsoft Word (.doc) format so you can start using them right away.

Your free bonus also includes a downloadable **Time Zone Meeting Coordination ebook** (a PDF file) that will help you schedule virtual team meetings across different time zones in seven easy steps. The ebook also comes with a **downloadable Excel spreadsheet template** that will save you time in creating your own.

To summarize, your free bonus includes the following four powerful tools:

* Meeting Agenda Template (MS Word .doc format)
* Meeting Minutes Template (MS Word .doc format)
* Time Zone Meeting Coordination ebook (Adobe .pdf format)
* Time Zone Meeting Coordination template (MS Excel .xls format)

Visit the following page to download your free bonus:

http://www.thecouchmanager.com/ivtbonus

Tactic #1: One Word That Influences Your Virtual Team

There's a famous experiment called the Xerox Study[1] that was conducted back in the late 1970s.

The idea was to discover if there was a best method for cutting in front of people who were waiting in line to use the photocopy machine.

Three requests were used (with different people at different times):

1. "Excuse me, I have five pages. May I use the Xerox machine, because I'm in a rush?"

2. "Excuse me, I have five pages. May I use the Xerox machine?"

3. "Excuse me, I have five pages. May I use the Xerox machine, because I have to make copies?"

The first request got a compliance rate of 94%. In other words, nearly everyone who was asked that question agreed to let the person use the photocopy machine ahead of them, maybe because they sympathized with the person who was in a rush.

The second request got a 60% rate of compliance. This decrease in compliance was probably because the

---

[1] Langer, Ellen J.; Blank, Arthur; Chanowitz, Benzion. "The Mindlessness of Ostensibly Thoughtful Action: The Role of "placebic" Information in Interpersonal Interaction." *Journal of Personality and Social Psychology* 36.6 (1978): 635-42. Print.

person who made the request didn't give a reason.

The third request got a rate of 93%, nearly as much as the first.

However, there is something unusual about that third request.

The reason given, "because I have to make copies," is ridiculous. Of course they needed to make copies! Why else would they ask?

It turns out that the study proved that it wasn't the reason that mattered in influencing people, but the use of the single word "because" that did.

In other words, using the word "because" increased the compliance rate by 33% regardless of what the justification was.

So the main lesson here is this:

Use the word "because" consistently to increase influence with your virtual team—in your emails, in your instant messages, in your meetings, and in your voice messages.

What comes after the word because doesn't matter, but try to make the reason credible.

Here are a couple of examples:

Example 1: "John, I need the status report by Thursday *because* I want to review it before Friday."

Example 2: "Sara, please schedule a meeting for next week *because* we have to discuss our strategy."

There you go—it's as simple as that.

Tactic #2: Set Deadlines

Most people are lazy.

They have an instinctive tendency to procrastinate with tasks that don't have a sense of urgency associated with them.

I know because I'm one of them.

I typically delay working on stuff whenever I get the chance.

Before starting on a task, I come up with false alibis such as waiting until I'm in a better mood or until I get more information.

There are many psychological reasons why people procrastinate, but a huge reason why we take forever to finish a task is something called Parkinson's Law.

Parkinson's Law states, "Work expands so as to fill the time available for its completion."

This means that if a task would typically require one hour to complete, and you assign a four-hour deadline to it, then it will take up the full four hours to get done.

In other words, if a task does *not* have a deadline associated with it, it will *never* get done.

That's the primary reason why you need to set deadlines with your team. It forces people to get things done.

But deadlines have other advantages in addition to avoiding Parkinson's Law from kicking in.

Deadlines develop a sense of urgency, hold team members accountable, provide a sense of encouragement, help in determining priorities, and provide a sense of accomplishment (after the deadlines are met).

They're a win-win for everyone. So use them.

But *how* do you set deadlines?

Here are three rules that you should keep in mind:

Rule 1: Be Reasonable

The first rule is to be reasonable about the timeframe of the deadline. If you know that a task needs a week to complete, then don't set a deadline for tomorrow.

This sounds obvious, but it is something that is commonly abused by managers. If you don't know how long a task would take, then simply ask for feedback. And if you're worried about not getting an honest answer, then ask for a best-case estimate and a worst-case estimate, and then average those two numbers out.

Rule 2: Be 100% Clear-Cut

The second rule is to be 100% clear-cut about when you want something done. Deadlines are ineffective if they're ambiguous. You need to mention the specific day, date, and time by which a task should be completed. If your team members live in different time zones, then mention the specific time zone as well.

So instead of the ambiguous "I need this done in the

next few days," you should say, "I need this done by Friday, June 9 at 3 p.m. US Eastern Time."

Rule 3: Always Set Deadlines

The third and final rule is to *always* set deadlines.

Every single task should have a deadline associated with it. Otherwise, Parkinson's Law takes over.

If you have a task that doesn't really need a deadline, then set one anyway by faking it (no one's going to really know the deadline is fake). And if the deadline is a few weeks out, then add an intermediate soft deadline as a checkpoint to make sure progress is being made on the task.

Again, *always* set deadlines.

Tactic #3: Assign Responsibility

Let me tell you the story of poor Kitty Genovese.

Kitty was a young woman who was stabbed to death in New York City back in 1964.

Over the course of half an hour, she was attacked three times on the street as neighbors watched from their windows.

There were thirty-eight witnesses to the horrific event, yet not a single person called the police during the attack.

The case caused a huge outcry in the news, and prompted psychologists to conduct a series of studies to understand why this happened.

They came up with a term for that phenomenon: the Bystander Effect.[2]

The bystander effect is the idea that in an emergency, the *greater* the number of bystanders, the *less likely* that anyone will help.

This is closely related to the *diffusion of responsibility* concept, where everyone's responsibility is no one's responsibility.

For Kitty, this meant that if there had been fewer witnesses, the odds would have been greater that one of

---

[2] Darley, John M., and Latané, Bibb. "Bystander intervention in emergencies: Diffusion of Responsibility." *Journal of Personality and Social Psychology* 8.4 (1968): 377–383. Print.

them would have taken action.

The main takeaway here for virtual teams is that if people are not willing to take action to help someone who is *dying* due to the bystander effect, then they will probably not take responsibility for assigned tasks in groups.

As a matter of fact, the bystander effect is compounded even further in virtual teams because of the lack of face-to-face interaction.

So to avoid the bystander effect in your team, you should always assign the responsibility of tasks to *specific* people.

Some managers tend to shy away from doing that, because they assume that someone in the team would just "pick the task up" and get it done. But that rarely happens.

Here are three tips that'll help you assign responsibility the right way:

Tip 1: Use Direct Language

First, you want to use direct language. This means using straight-to-the-point language that tells people *exactly* who is responsible for getting things done. This avoids any confusion about who's responsible.

For example, if you say, "David, I think we should work on this task," you're using indirect language because the words "think" and "we" makes it seem like you're only alluding to the fact that David needs to work on the task. But he might not pick up on that.

However, if you say, "David, I need *you* to work on this task," you're using direct language and avoiding any confusion about the fact that you want David to work on the assignment.

Tip 2: Ask for Volunteers

The second tip is to ask for volunteers. When a task could be accomplished by several members of a team, asking for volunteers has a couple of advantages.

First, when someone volunteers, the chances of the task getting done increases because of an influence principle called commitment and consistency.[3] This means that to remain consistent with their own internal self-image, people are more likely to honor a commitment that they signed up for rather than one that was assigned.

Second, it gives people the chance to work on what they want to work on, which creates happier (translation: more productive) team members.

However, if the situation or the task does not allow for volunteers (or if no one volunteers), then you should still assign responsibility to someone.

Tip 3: Assign to Individuals

The third tip is to make sure you assign to individuals and not to groups. Assigning tasks to more than one person will still create a bystander effect within that small group.

---

[3] Cialdini, Robert B. "Chapter 3: Commitment and Consistency." *Influence: The Psychology of Persuasion.* New York: Collins, 2007. Print.

If a task requires more than one person to work on it, then assign the primary responsibility to a specific person, and the secondary responsibility to others.

So instead of saying "Karen, Jessica, and Steve will be responsible for completing this task," you should say, "Karen will be responsible for completing this task, and both Jessica and Steve will help her out."

Tactic #4: Explain Tasks

Thorkil Sonne is the founder of Specialisterne, a software company in Denmark. The name means "the specialists."

The company is well known around the world because it makes millions of dollars in revenue by employing people with autism.

Autism is a developmental disability that is typically characterized by communication difficulties and social impairments.

It's a spectrum disorder that affects millions of people around the world, and you typically wouldn't find people with autism working in a regular job, not to mention a software development company.

So what Sonne did was extraordinary, and he received a lot of awards and media attention about his accomplishments as a social entrepreneur.

When Sonne was asked by the *Harvard Business Review*,[4] "How does managing autistic workers differ from managing other people?" this was his answer:

"[Our consultants with autism] have trouble... understanding social cues, such as gestures, facial expressions, and tone of voice. You have to be precise and direct with them, be very specific about your expectations, and avoid sarcasm and nonverbal

[4] Donovan, Susan. "Entrepreneur Thorkil Sonne on what you can learn from employees with autism." *Harvard Business Review*. Sep 2008: 1. Print. [Reprint F0809F]

communication."

I think virtual teams should be managed the same way.

If I wanted to summarize the absolute best way to communicate with virtual teams (particularly global teams) to avoid ambiguity and confusion, I would use the exact same words Sonne used:

Virtual teams have trouble understanding social cues, such as gestures, facial expressions, and tone of voice. You have to be precise and direct with them, be very specific about your expectations, and avoid sarcasm and nonverbal communication.

Here are two strategies to help you accomplish that.

Strategy 1: Know What You Want

First, make sure that you know exactly what you want. While this seems obvious, one of the biggest causes of miscommunication among virtual teams is that managers don't really know what they want, even if they think they do.

So before asking for a specific task, you want to be 100% clear within yourself about what you want. Otherwise, you will just confuse your team.

Strategy 2: Be Direct in Your Description

The second strategy is to be as direct as possible with your task description. You should get to the point as fast as you can, and say exactly what you want by using the right words, without leaving anything open to interpretation or assumptions.

So instead of saying, "Please write a brief summary report about the status of our project," you should say, "Please send me a one-slide PowerPoint presentation that summarizes the status of our project in a few bullet points."

Tactic #5: When Delegating Tasks, Write Them Out

The one thing you should always do when delegating is to write out the tasks.

That's because there's a mysterious power in writing.

In *Bargaining for Advantage*,[5] Professor G. Richard Shell gives a remarkable example about that from an old hidden camera TV show, where producers placed a fake sign on the highway between Pennsylvania and Delaware that read "DELAWARE CLOSED."

Some of the drivers who were driving to Delaware ignored the sign, but a few others stopped, believed it, and turned around.

One concerned driver even asked, "When do you think it will reopen? I live there, and my family is in there!"

That's how powerful a printed phrase can be. This is due to something called the "deference to authority" principle, where printed words carry a much higher authoritative message than verbal ones.

That's why writing tasks down will dramatically increase the probability that they will get done by your virtual team.

Here are a couple of rules to make this effective.

---

[5] Shell, G. Richard. "The Power of Authority." *Bargaining for advantage: negotiating strategies for reasonable people.* 2nd ed. New York: Penguin Books, 2006. Print.

Rule 1: Type the Task Message in Real Time

The first rule is to type out your tasks while your virtual team is watching you during a conference call. This is the absolute best way to get a commitment from someone and increase adoption rates.

This means typing out tasks over web-sharing software (such as WebEx Meetings or GoToMeeting) where participants see you typing exactly what needs to be done on a spreadsheet or presentation slide.

Even if they can't see you, just *sounding* like you're typing out the task over a teleconference call will have a similar powerful effect (say something like "Hold on while I write this down...").

Rule 2: Always Type Out Verbal Tasks

The second rule is to always type out the tasks and send them to your team. Don't rely on verbal task requests—not even minor ones.

You could type tasks on a shared online space, a meeting minutes document, a spreadsheet, or even an email. It doesn't matter.

They key is to have them typed out *somewhere*, and not depend on verbal assignments.

Even if you *really* trust that your team members will follow your verbal instructions, writing tasks down will help them remember the tasks, have a reference point to go back to, and avoid any potential miscommunication.

Tactic #6: The Secret Formula for Establishing Trust

In any successful virtual team, one of the primary prerequisites to get someone to do what you need them to do is to establish trust between you and them.

But what is trust?

Here's one definition: trust is the "assured reliance on the character, ability, strength, or truth of someone or something."[6]

Although this is a good definition, trust is still a nebulous concept because it is not tangible.

You cannot see it, hear it, or quantify it.

Plus, trust is not like an on/off light switch. You can't *have* trust or *not have* trust within a team.

Trust is more like a spectrum, where you have varying degrees of trust that range from very low to very high.

This makes it trickier to manage.

Nevertheless, creating a high degree of trust in a virtual environment is vital to the success of the team because individuals who trust each other produce more.

Moreover, a low degree of trust results in a lack of

---

[6] "Trust." Merriam-Webster.com. Merriam-Webster, n.d. Web. 12 June 2014. <http://www.merriam-webster.com/dictionary/trust>.

commitment, poor team performance, and negative energy among the team.

Because there can be many factors involved, such as cultures, personalities, communication, and dispersion, establishing trust can be a complicated process.

However, developing and building trust among a virtual team can be accomplished by following a methodical process.

First, let me give you the secret formula for trust that will help guide you with your strategy of keeping trust high among your team.

Here it is:

Trust = Reliability + Likeability

That's it.

Trust is equal to the level of reliability plus the level of likeability.

So to *increase* trust among the team, you need to increase the level of reliability or increase the level of likeability, or both.

In the next couple of sections, I'll show you exactly how to do that.

Tactic #7: Increase Reliability Among Your Team

In the previous section, we talked about the secret formula for trust being Trust = Reliability + Likeability, and that to increase trust, we need to increase reliability or likeability, or both.

This section is about how to increase reliability.

What is reliability?

Reliability is basically the ability and dependability of a team member to accomplish a task according to pre-defined objectives.

This is usually referred to by psychologists as the *cognitive trust* component, and it is a function of a person's ability and integrity.* [7]

In other words, it answers the question: can the person get the job done in a reliable way?

Here are the four steps to increase reliability among your team:

Step 1: Verify Skills

The main root cause of a lack of reliability among virtual teams is a lack of proper team skills, so the first step

---

[7] Greenberg, Penelope Sue, Ralph H. Greenberg, and Yvonne Lederer Antonucci. "Creating and Sustaining Trust in Virtual Teams." *Business Horizons* 50.4 (2007): 325-33. Web.

you should do is verify them.

There are two types of skills: technical skills and collaboration skills.

Technical Skills are the skills needed to do the job itself (e.g., software development skills or engineering skills).

Collaboration skills are skills needed to interact and communicate in a virtual environment (e.g., virtual technology or communication skills). Those skills are sometimes considered a part of your typical "soft" skills.

Both types of skills are essential to make sure that there is a high degree of reliability among your team, and you should verify both of them with your team members before they start their roles.

Some questions you can ask your team members when assessing their skills include: "Are you comfortable doing this task?" or "Do you have any concerns about this project?"

Step 2: Be Explicit

The second tactic is to be as explicit as you can with expectations and requests when communicating with your team.

You cannot rely on someone to do a task if they're not 100% clear on what they have to do. So say exactly what you want (and when you want it), and don't leave requests open to interpretation or assumptions.

You also want to keep communicating throughout the task's timeframe to make sure there are no misunderstandings.

Step 3: Lead by Example

The third tactic to increase reliability is to set an example of how reliable *you* are to your own virtual team.

This is because your team actually looks up to your behavior as the standard reference point of how they should behave.

If you're not reliable with your own commitments, you implicitly give your team permission to behave accordingly.

In short: Lead by example. When you say you will do something, do it.

Step 4: Count on Others

The fourth tactic is to count on others to do their job.

Although this might sound counterintuitive, counting on others to do their job will increase their level of reliability.

Research shows that "a propensity to believe others can be counted on to do what they say they will do is an important precursor to the development of trust."[8]

Show your team members that you trust them, and they'll become more reliable.

---

[8] Greenberg, Penelope Sue, Ralph H. Greenberg, and Yvonne Lederer Antonucci. "Creating and Sustaining Trust in Virtual Teams." *Business Horizons* 50.4 (2007): 325-33. Web.

Keep in mind that no matter how much you try increasing the level of reliability among your team, there are certain people who are just poor performers.

Those individuals will affect the entire team by free-riding, and create a negative environment of distrust.

You can try addressing poor performance issues by having honest conversations about conduct, but understand that there's only so much you can do, and sometimes, letting team members go is the best solution for you and the team.

Tactic #8: Increase the Level of Likeability

A couple of sections ago, we talked about the secret formula for trust being: Trust = Reliability + Likeability, and that to increase trust, we need to increase reliability or likeability, or both.

The previous section was about how to increase reliability. This section is about how to increase likeability.

What is likeability?

Likeability is the forming of emotional ties between members of a team, and is the result of social bonds developed in a reciprocal relationship between two people.

It is usually referred to as the *affective trust* component, which is based on assessments of benevolence.[9]

In other words, it answers the question: "Do I like the person enough to trust that they'd do the job?"

So how do you increase likeability?

Likeability in a virtual team can be increased similar to how it's increased in co-located teams, but it takes a little more effort and time.

---

[9] Greenberg, Penelope Sue, Ralph H. Greenberg, and Yvonne Lederer Antonucci. "Creating and Sustaining Trust in Virtual Teams." *Business Horizons* 50.4 (2007): 325-33. Web.

Here are five steps that will help you.

Step 1: Get Personal

The first tactic is to get personal. Virtual teams can sometimes feel very transactional and dry because everyone is usually focused on completing their tasks and getting their job done.

However, getting to know your team members on a personal level is one of the fastest ways to increase likeability.

You can accomplish that by learning about your team members' families, vacation plans, and hobbies through informal discussions.

Leading by example works here as well. If you share personal anecdotes about yourself, then your team will feel more at ease about opening up to you.

Important side note here: make sure you don't violate any local laws or company policies when asking personal questions. Keep in mind that even though it's probably OK to ask high-level personal questions, you don't want to get too intrusive. And stay away from discussing religion or politics - those are always sensitive topics.

Step 2: Encourage Social Interactions

One major drawback of virtual teams is that they lack the "water cooler" effect, where employees in a physical office typically gather around a water cooler to chat.

Encouraging social interactions will help you create a

virtual water cooler to increase team likeability and cohesion among your team.

One way to accomplish that is to start or end conversations you have in meetings that are unrelated to work. Spending a few minutes upfront talking about anything informal is a great way to break the ice and get everyone talking.

Another strategy is to use the power of small gives, where you can share articles, videos or events (through email or Instant Messaging) that you think your team members might be interested in.

This creates a nice degree of intimacy and cohesion among your team.

Finally, you can also schedule separate meetings (or portions of meetings) that are dedicated to team building or team bonding exercises.

Step 3: Over-Communicate

The third step to increase likeability is to "over-communicate" with your team. In other words, you need to regularly interact with them.

This is based on a theory developed by psychologists at MIT called the "Propinquity Effect," which states that the more you interact with someone, the more you'll like them and become friends with them.

Repeat exposure through over communication among your team will eventually lead to an increase in liking.

So stay in touch with your team members at least once every day (or every other day), even if it's not absolutely essential.

An easy way to do this is to connect with them using Instant Messaging software, or give them a quick call every once in a while to check on things.

Step 4: Meet Face to Face

Meeting with your team members face to face at least once (especially right after a project starts), is the single best thing you can do to increase liking among your team.

Face to face meetings help with establishing rapport, understanding mannerisms, and reducing miscommunication.

Although bringing a team together in one room could be a large expense if your team is widely distributed, it is still worth it down the line, particularly in long-term projects.

However, if meeting face to face is not possible due to budgetary or other constraints, then using video conferencing as a secondary option definitely helps.

Step 5: Be Positive

The final tactic to increase likeability is to be positive with your attitude.

No one enjoys working with individuals who are constantly negative and pessimistic.

Although it is quite natural to go through some high-stress times while working in virtual teams, what matters is how you react during those times with your team.

Having a constant positive attitude (and encouraging others to do the same) will increase the level of likeability among the team.

In summary, you can increase the level of trust within your team by increasing the level of reliability and likeability.

To increase reliability, make sure you (1) verify skills (2) be explicit (3) lead by example, and (4) count on others.

And to increase likeability, you should (1) get personal (2) encourage social interactions (3) over-communicate (4) meet face to face and (5) be positive.

Tactic #9: Six Steps to Ensure 100% Commitment

For really important tasks—those that you absolutely need to get done no matter what—there is a methodical step-by-step process that ensures 100% commitment by the person who is assigned to the task.

This six-step process[10] builds on some of the previous tactics that I mentioned, but it's the combination of those tactics that makes this process very effective.

However, make sure you use this process sparingly, because overusing it could backfire and your team members might become immune to it. So reserve using it for those tasks that you really need to get done.

Step 1: Ask Them to Repeat It Back to You

After you assign an action to someone, ask them to say the task or repeat it back to you. Having them say the words substantially increases their sense of understanding and commitment to the task.

For example, at the end of a meeting or conversation, say something like "Just to make sure, I'd like to confirm what everyone is going to be working on next."

---

[10] Adapted from: Lieberman, David J., *Get Anyone to Do Anything: Never Feel Powerless Again -- with Psychological Secrets to Control and Influence Every Situation.* New York: St. Martin's Griffin, 2001. Print.

Step 2: Get a Time Frame

If you've already assigned a deadline to the task, then ask the person to repeat or confirm that as well (for example, "You said you'll get that done by this Friday, correct?")

If you have not assigned a deadline to the task, then ask how long it would take for them to complete the task (again, you should *always* have a deadline).

For example, after getting confirmation about a task, say something like "Great, so when will you be able to get that done?" or "Any idea of how long that will take you?"

Step 3: Develop an Obligation

The next step is to develop a sense of obligation to let the person know that because of their help, you will be altering your original plans.

The idea is to let the person understand that a withdrawal of their commitment will result in some sort of a disturbance to you.

This creates an even higher incentive for them to get the task done because the stakes are now greater.

Here's an example of what you can say: "Ok then—I'll move my other scheduled appointments to make sure I'm free on that day to discuss the draft."

Step 4: Stress Importance

The next step is to develop a *sense of conscience* to let

the person know that you are now *dependent* on them to get the task done.

You want to stress the importance of the task as well as the negative consequences that might occur if it doesn't get done.

Here's an example of what you can say: "Hey Dave, just as a side note, I will get reprimanded publicly if this isn't done by Tuesday, so it's really important!"

Step 5: Confirm Action

The next step is to close the request by *confirming* that the action will be carried out.

End the meeting or conversation using a solid and concise verbal confirmation phrase.

Here's an example of what you can say when you end the conversation: "So I'll definitely be getting a copy of this on Friday, right?"

Part of this step is to also write the task out and send it in a summary email after the meeting.

Step 6: Show Appreciation

A day or so after you make the request (and sometime before the due date of the task approaches), follow-up with the person by expressing appreciation.

Let the person know how much you value their efforts of following through on a task and that they're the kind of person who gets the job done.

This not only reminds them of the task, but also appeals to their own sense of internal commitment to reinforce their dedication to the action item.

For example, say something like, "Sarah, I really appreciate your help on this task being done by Wednesday—you're one of a few people who I can count on getting this done."

To recap, the six-step process is as follows: (1) Ask them to repeat it back to you (2) Get a time frame (3) Develop an obligation (4) Stress importance (5) Confirm action, and (6) Show appreciation.

Tactic #10: Know What Someone Is Really Thinking

Knowing what someone on your team is really thinking about something is a powerful thing.

It gives you tremendous leverage because you'll understand any underlying motives by your team members.

However, it is a challenge to know exactly what someone's thoughts are about a task, a project or a deliverable.

For a million different reasons, your team members might give you an untruthful answer.

So if you ask a question like, "What do you really think about this?" you would probably not get the answer you're looking for.

However, there is a two-step process[11] that never fails to let you know exactly what someone is really thinking.

The first step is to isolate them, and the second is to ask them one of four questions.

---

[11] Adapted from: Lieberman, David J. *Get Anyone to Do Anything: Never Feel Powerless Again-- with Psychological Secrets to Control and Influence Every Situation.* New York: St. Martin's Griffin, 2001. Print.

Step 1: Isolate Them

The best way to make someone comfortable about speaking freely is to isolate them from the rest of the team.

This helps put them at ease because they'll have fewer people who will listen to what they have to say, and it also avoids any political motives from interfering with their answer.

In a virtual environment, this means scheduling a separate one-on-one call with that person to discuss the topic.

Step 2: Ask Them One of Four Questions

After you isolate them, there are four questions you can ask them to find out what they are really thinking:

1) What would it take for you to *love* this task (or project)?
2) How do you think I can make this *better*?
3) What would it take for you to be *really excited* about this?
4) What would you do *differently*?

Those questions work because they all do a couple of things.

First, they inherently assume that the person accepts the task and therefore makes them more comfortable about criticizing it.

And second, they reveal an acknowledgment that nothing is perfect, which makes it easier for someone to offer their real thoughts.

Try out these questions—they never fail.

Tactic #11: Leave the Perfect Voice Message

In a virtual team, you always want to leave the perfect voice message for several reasons.

First, you want to make sure you get your message across clearly and minimize any potential miscommunication. And second, you want to avoid what's called "phone tag syndrome," where you call someone and leave a message, they call back and leave a message, you call back, and so on.

The idea is to create a "one-shot, one-kill" self-sustaining voice message that gives the recipient *everything* they need to know without the need for them to get back to you for clarification.

In short, they should know *why you're calling, what you need them to do,* and *how they can reach you.*

The best way to show you what the perfect voice message includes is to give you an example of one and break it down for you.

Here it is:

"Hello Sara. **[1]** This is David Wilson from Globex. **[2]** It is 1:00 p.m. on Thursday, July 16 **[3]** and I'm calling to let you know that I'm ready to ship your laptop battery. **[4]** After you get this message, please call me back so I can confirm your address. **[5]** You can reach me at 617-555-3962 anytime between 8:00 a.m. and 5:00 p.m. Eastern Time. **[6]** Again, my number is 617-555-3962. **[7]** Thank you!"

[1] Say their name: "Hello Sara." Say your recipient's name in the greeting; it'll grab their attention. This will also minimize the possibility they think you're some random caller, especially if they don't know your voice.

[2] Give your info: "This is David Wilson from Globex." Say your name (and if you're calling a business client, the company you work for). Make sure it's your full name; there are millions of Davids in this world.

[3] State the time and date: "It is 1:00 p.m. on Thursday, July 16." Nearly all phone services have the option to retrieve the time you called someone, but no one has the patience to go through that menu, so do the person a favor and tell them when you called in case they got the message later in the day or the next morning.

[4] Explain the objective: "I'm calling to let you know that I'm ready to ship your laptop battery." State the reason why you're calling and what you want to let the person know. Be concise; no one wants to hear a long story here.

[5] Explain the action item: "Please call me back so I can confirm your address." Do you want them to call you back ASAP? Do you want them to email you instead? Do you want them to create a report and send it before the next day? Always have an action item, or state a lack thereof.

[6] Leave your number: "You can reach me at 617-555-3962 anytime between 8:00 a.m. and 5:00 p.m. Eastern Time." Even if you don't think the person you're calling should call you back, always leave your number—they might need it. E-N-U-N-C-I-A-T-E and speak slowly. You can also mention when it's best to call you back and the time zone you're in, if you have a preference.

[7] Leave your number a second time: "Again, my number is 617-555-3962." Chances are that even though you spoke slowly the first time, the person would have missed writing your number down. Although they can replay the voice message to hear it again, you'll win some points if you repeat it for them at the end.

By ensuring that you have all those seven parts in every voice message, you'll guarantee that your recipients will have everything they need to take action.

Tactic #12: Write Assertive Emails

To sound assertive in your email messages and make sure that you influence your team get things done, you need to do a couple of things.

First, you need to keep your emails short and concise, and second, you need to highlight your calls to action within your emails.

Step 1: Keep Emails Short and Concise

Here's a quick fact: No one reads long emails anymore. People just scan them.

So if you want someone to read your email, you should keep your message as short and as simple as possible. You should also try to get to the point of your email early on in your message—preferably in the first paragraph—so that you don't waste your recipient's time with any fluff.

According to research from Carnegie Mellon University, emails that are easy to address get answered faster.[12]

So if you keep your messages short and sweet, you'll gain the advantage that they will be addressed quickly.

---

[12] Dabbish, Laura A., Robert E. Kraut, Susan Fussell, and Sara Kiesler. "Understanding Email Use: Predicting Action on a Message." *Proceedings of the SIGCHI Conference on Human Factors in Computing Systems* (2005): 691-700. Carnegie Mellon University. Web.

Step 2: Highlight Your Calls to Action

Calls to action are the action items or tasks that you want your email recipients to accomplish (which, as discussed in the previous sections, should be assigned to a single person and have always a deadline associated with them).

Because people scan emails, you should avoid burying your calls to action in multiple paragraphs. A best practice is to highlight them so that they are easily identifiable within the email.

My default method is to list each call to action out in a separate bullet point.

However, you can also use **bolding**, *italicizing*, underlining, or different color fonts to draw attention to the action items.

Tactic #13: What You Should Do *Before* Every Meeting

I hate meetings.

I think that nine times out of ten they're a waste of time.

There are two main problems with meetings.

First, we attend too many meetings (a quantity problem), and second, we attend too many *bad* meetings (a quality problem).

However, I think meetings are useful if managed the right way. Virtual meetings can be essential for getting people on the same page when things get confusing, and in terms of getting things done, they can be instrumental in keeping your level of influence high.

In the next couple of sections, I'll explain what you need to do before, during, and after each meeting so that you reduce both the quality and quantity problems with your meetings.

You'll also learn how to increase the level of influence with your team members to get things done.

Quick side note here: I know that meetings is a boring subject, but meetings are the second worst time wasters in your work life (the first is email), so do take this topic seriously. If you follow these steps to the letter, you'll never need to read anything else about meetings again.

Let's start with the five things you need to do *before* every virtual meeting you facilitate:

Step 1: Decide On a Need

The first question you should ask yourself before setting up any meeting is: "Do I really need to have this meeting?"

Think really, really hard about that question, and about whether you can write an email, set up a quick call, or use some other channel instead of having a meeting with your team.

Chances are you can use any of those alternatives instead.

As someone once said, "Just like wars, meetings should be a last resort."

Step 2: Define the Objective

Every meeting must have an objective.

And the objective should be determined *before* you set up the meeting, not during. If you're having difficulty defining a goal for the meeting, then see Step 1. You probably don't need one.

To define an objective, simply complete this sentence: "The objective of this meeting is to _____ "

And fill in the blank with a phrase that starts with an action verb:

"make a decision on..."
"generate ideas about..."
"get status on..."

"make plans for..."

Step 3: Determine the Attendees

The next step is to think about whom to invite to your meeting.

Individuals are often invited just to "stay in the loop." They don't have any functional reason to be there.

I've been on meetings where there were over twenty people invited, but the conversation was applicable to only three of them.

That's not only a waste of time, but you'll essentially decrease the level of influence you can have over such a fragmented group.

The general heuristic is that you want to limit the number of attendees so that you can have a very focused and effective meeting that maximizes your chances of getting things done.

Step 4: Draft an Agenda

Every meeting should have an agenda that explains exactly what the meeting is about.

Most people think an agenda should be a fancy or a formal document, but it doesn't have to be.

It could be just a couple of bullet points or a short paragraph.

When you're writing the agenda, start it out with the objective (which you defined in Step 2 above), and then list out the discussion points you want to focus on.

Begin your list with the top priorities first—the important stuff that absolutely must be covered in your meeting—and then move on to the least important items.

You can also highlight who will talk about what, and set time limits for each topic. I usually don't do that unless I'm dealing with a very large team and need to keep a tight level of control on my meeting. So you can skip the name assignments and time limits if you're leading a smaller team.

Side note: In the beginning of the book, I mentioned that I've included a free meeting agenda template (in MS word format) that you can download and use with your own team. Here's the link again if you haven't downloaded it:

http://www.thecouchmanager.com/ivtbonus

Step 5: Send the Invite, Agenda, and Reminders

The last step is to send out the meeting invite along with the agenda so that your team has time to prepare for the meeting.

As you get closer to the meeting date, you might want to send out follow-up reminders so that your attendees can go over any material you want them to review prior to the meeting.

Say something like, "To have an effective meeting and not waste everyone's time, please make sure you review the report and come up with potential solutions *before* you show up to the meeting on Friday."

Those five steps might seem elementary, but if you're having meetings that don't produce results, follow these steps—and the next two sections—carefully.

Tactic #14: What You Should Do *During* Every Meeting

To keep things focused and gain buy-in, here are the five things you need to do during every virtual meeting.

Step 1: Appoint a Leader

No leader = a waste of time.

Every meeting should have a designated leader who is responsible for moderating the meeting, achieving the stated objectives, and capturing any notes.

Normally, that leader would be you (as the manager of the virtual team), but in some cases, you might assign that role to someone else.

Step 2: Go Through the Agenda

When you (the leader) begin the meeting, you should start by talking about the objective and state the outcome you want to achieve from that meeting ("The objective of this meeting is to...").

Then walk through the rest of the agenda and explain to your team members what you expect them to talk about or discuss.

Step 3: Remain on Topic (and Time)

As you go through the meeting, stick to the agenda

items and hold people accountable for their time limits. Don't let anyone stray off in a different direction.

Use the agenda as an alibi to make sure everyone remains on topic, and ask individuals to take any side conversations offline. This is obvious, but few leaders do it.

Also, if anyone joins late, avoid repeating information. Carry on with your meeting. The latecomer can be brought up to speed later through the meeting minutes.

Step 4: Capture Meeting Minutes

No documentation = useless meeting.

Focus on capturing these three significant points during every meeting:
1) Risks are problems that you might encounter in the future.

2) Issues are problems you are currently encountering.

3) Action items are the tasks that the team needs to work on next (which could be related to a risk or an issue).

Assign owners to each specific risk, issue, or action, and set deadlines for actions.

Also, capture notes of any decisions or ideas that have been discussed in the meeting.

Side note: The free bonus I referred to at the beginning of the book also includes a sample meeting minutes template (in MS word format) that you can copy & paste and use with your team.

Step 5: Close with a Review

A few minutes before the meeting ends, do a full review of the notes you took.

Start with the action items first, and verbally confirm the tasks with the assigned owners and mention the deadlines.

Then, if you have some time remaining, go over the risks, issues, and any other decisions or ideas that were discussed.

Summarizing what was said in the meeting is the best way to increase the chances that things will get done, and ensure there is no confusion among the team about who's doing what.

Tactic #15: What You Should Do *After* Every Meeting

Here are the two things you need to do after every virtual meeting:

Step 1: Distribute Meeting Minutes

After the meeting is over, distribute the meeting minutes to everyone who attended the meeting and anyone who missed it so that every team member has a reference point to go back to.

You could also upload the meeting minutes to a document repository for future reference.

While there's some debate about whether meeting minutes are effective (most people don't really read them), they might be necessary (or even required) in some projects to track issues if they surface later on.

Step 2: Follow-Up With a Written Summary

After the meeting is over, you should *always* follow up with a written summary that highlights specifically who is working on what and when everything is due.

Although those action items would already be listed in the meeting minutes document that you distributed, there are many benefits in highlighting them separately in an email.

One best practice is to send out an email with an action

list and include the meeting minutes as an attachment (in MS Word or PDF) to minimize the number of emails you send out.

Summary of Action Steps Before, During, and After Each Meeting

To summarize, here's what you should do before every meeting:

1. Decide on a need
2. Define the objective
3. Determine the attendees
4. Draft an agenda
5. Send the invite, agenda and reminders

Here's what you should do during each meeting:

1. Have a leader
2. Go through the agenda
3. Remain on topic (and time)
4. Capture meeting minutes
5. Close with a review

And finally, here's what you should do after each meeting:

1. Distribute meeting minutes
2. Follow up with a summary

If you follow those steps with each team meeting, you will have fewer meetings, you'll have better meetings, and you and your team will live happily ever after.

Tactic #16: Use Your Voice to Your Advantage

There are two things that matter in any meeting, presentation or phone conversation with your team members:

The first is what you say (the content), and the second is how you say it (your voice).

In terms of engaging and influencing your team, especially in a virtual environment, *how* you say something, or your vocal quality, can sometimes be more important than *what* you say.

You can have the best content under the sun, but if you don't use the proper verbal delivery mechanism, you will lose your audience's attention.

Here are four tips you should focus on that will give you an advantage when you talk to your team.

Tip 1: Tone

The tone of your voice includes all its vocal features, such as pitch, quality, and volume.

If you talk in a monotonous, low-pitch, and low-volume voice, then regardless of how exciting the topic is, some people on your team are going to doze off.

A good tone of voice is one that has a good level of energy to it and reflects confidence: the quality is clear, the volume is moderate, and the pitch has a nice vocal range to it.

One way to know how good your tone of voice sounds is to record yourself during a meeting, and then listen to the recording afterward.

Tip 2: Speed

The speed of your voice is about how fast you talk.

If you speak at too fast a pace, then your listeners might miss out on what you have to say because they wouldn't have enough time to absorb your message.

If you talk at too slow a pace, then your listeners might get bored.

A moderate and solid pace is the best speed at which you should talk for your team to catch up with you and actively listen to what you have to say.

Tip 3: Enunciation

Enunciation means pronouncing a word or a phrase clearly.

Different people have different accents (particularly when you're working with global teams), and what might sound right to you could be confusing to your team.

So put in the extra effort to say certain words that might be misconstrued, especially if you work in a field like technology, medicine, engineering or law, where there are a lot of technical words.

In addition, when you spell an acronym or word in a

virtual setting, there are certain letters can easily be mixed up (such as "B" and "P") because they sound the same over the phone.

To avoid that problem, use a spelling alphabet, which is a set of words that represent the different letters.

The most common spelling alphabet system is the NATO phonetic alphabet (see the list here: *http://en.wikipedia.org/wiki/NATO_phonetic_alphabet*)

For example, to pronounce "ASV9" using the NATO phonetic alphabet, you would say "A as in Alfa, S as in Sierra, V as in Victor, and 9 as in Niner."

Go slow and be forceful with each letter and number.

Tip 4: Silence

The last thing you should use to give yourself an advantage with your voice is silence.

Silence is about injecting intentional pauses in your discussion.

Most people think silence is a bad thing, so they fill up their speech with random filler words like "um," "you know?" "er" and "ok," which can get very distracting.

However, silence can actually help because it gives your listeners some breathing room to digest your message.

It also helps in grabbing your team's attention when you need to discuss something important.

Throughout your verbal discussions, inject silence to emphasize something or to give your audience some time to absorb your content.

To recap, if you use a solid tone of voice, a moderate speed, and you enunciate important words while using silence in your discussions, you will sound more authoritative and have much more influence over your team.

Tactic #17: Make Your Emails Stand Out Using The Subject Line

According to one McKinsey study,[13] the average worker spends over twenty-eight percent of their workweek managing email.

So if you work forty hours a week, that means you're spending over eleven hours per week *on email alone.*

Some managers receive up to three hundred emails a day (and those don't even include spam!).

If you want your email messages to stand out from the crowd and get addressed promptly, you have to think like a marketer, especially with your subject line.

Here are three things to include in your subject line to make someone reply to your emails:

Step 1: Write Their Name

People are primed to recognize their name when they skim over it in a bunch of junk, so start out the subject of the email with their first name. Using their nickname earns you higher points.

---

[13] Chui, Michael, James Manyika, Jacques Bughin, Richard Dobbs, Charles Roxburgh, Hugo Sarrazin, Geoffrey Sands, and Magdalena Westergren. "The Social Economy: Unlocking Value and Productivity through Social Technologies." *McKinsey & Company.* McKinsey Global Institute, July 2012. Web. 12 June 2014.

Step 2: Summarize the Email's Topic

Include a summary of your email's message. Think about the objective you're trying to achieve, and don't just type a generic summary (e.g., "Resume Attached"). If your objective is to get an answer, then ask a question (e.g., "Think this attached resume sounds like a good candidate for the job?").

Step 3: Write Down a Deadline

As I mentioned earlier, deadlines create a powerful sense of urgency, and people dislike missing them. So state the deadline in your subject line as well.

Here are a couple of good/bad subject line examples:

Bad Example: Status Update Deck
Good Example: Justin – I need your input on this status update deck by tomorrow @ 6:00 p.m.

Bad Example: Lunch
Good Example: Jen – are you available this Thu for lunch? Let me know by COB

Conclusion

We've covered seventeen killer tactics that'll help you motivate your virtual team to be more productive.

Some of those tactics can be applied immediately, while others need a bit of time to be implemented with your remote employees.

My first suggestion is to go back to the beginning of the book and re-read the first five tactics. These will give you the greatest impact in the shortest amount of time.

Tactic 1 was about using the word "because." This is a super-simple tip that you can start using right away which will instantly increase the compliance rate by your team.

Tactics 2, 3, 4, and 5 were about setting specific deadlines, assigning responsibility the right way, explaining tasks clearly, and always writing things down. Those four tactics, when used together, will fundamentally shift the way in which you run your team.

After reviewing those tactics, identify the other tactics that you'd like to use based on your own situation. Here are a few suggestions that will help you out:

**Understand how to increase trust (Tactics 6, 7 and 8).
**What to do before, during, and after each meeting (Tactics 13, 14, and 15).
**How to use email effectively (Tactics 12 and 17).
**How to use your voice effectively (Tactics 11 and 16).
**How to know what someone is really thinking (Tactic 10).

Implementing all those tactics will help you manage your virtual team more effectively, increase their productivity, and help you to lead a stress-free and happy professional life.

Thank You!

I'd like to thank you once again for purchasing my book. I hope you found it helpful, and I wish you the best of luck with managing your virtual team.

I know there are a lot of other books about virtual teams, and the fact that you chose this one and read all the way to the end means a lot to me.

I'd like to ask you for a small favor.

If you enjoyed the book, I'd be very grateful if you leave an honest review on Amazon (I read them all).

Every single review counts, and your support really does make a difference.

Thanks again for your kind support!

Cheers,

Hassan

Made in the USA
San Bernardino, CA
08 May 2020